It Doesn't Grow on Trees

Sources of Income

By Diane Dakers

Educational Consultant:
Christopher A. Fons, M.A.
Social Studies and Economics Faculty
Milwaukee Public Schools

Crabtree Publishing Company
www.crabtreebooks.com

Financial
Literacy
for Life

Author: Diane Dakers

Series research and development: Reagan Miller

Project coordinator: Mark Sachner, Water Buffalo Books

Editorial director: Kathy Middleton

Editors: Mark Sachner, Janine Deschenes

Proofreader: Wendy Scavuzzo

Photo research: Westgraphix/Tammy West

Designer: Westgraphix/Tammy West

Production coordinator and prepress technician:
  Tammy McGarr

Print coordinator: Margaret Amy Salter

Contributing writer and editor: Christopher A. Fons,
economics teacher, Riverside University High School,
Milwaukee Public Schools

Written and produced for Crabtree Publishing Company by
Water Buffalo Books

Photographs:

Front cover: All images from Shutterstock

Interior:
Shutterstock: pp. 1, 3, 4, 5, 6, 7, 8, 9, 10, 11, 12, 13, 14, 15, 16,
    18, 19, 20, 21 (top), 22 (top), 23, 24, 25, 26, 27, 29, 31, 32, 33,
    34 (top; bottom: upper left and lower center), 35, 36, 37, 39, 41,
    43; cjmacer: p. 28; lev radin: p. 21 (bottom); Radiokafka: p. 22
    (bottom).
Water Buffalo Books: p. 34 (bottom: upper right).

Library and Archives Canada Cataloguing in Publication

Dakers, Diane, author
        It doesn't grow on trees : sources of income / Diane Dakers.

(Financial literacy for life)
Includes index.
Issued in print and electronic formats.
ISBN 978-0-7787-3096-5 (hardcover).--
ISBN 978-0-7787-3105-4 (softcover).--
ISBN 978-1-4271-1875-2 (HTML)

        1. Finance, Personal--Juvenile literature. 2. Saving and investment--
Juvenile literature. 3. Income--Juvenile literature. 4. Investments--Juvenile
literature. 5. Loans--Juvenile literature. I. Title.

HG179.D3434 2017   j332.024   C2016-907139-1
                                                     C2016-907140-5

Library of Congress Cataloging-in-Publication Data

CIP available at the Library of Congress

Crabtree Publishing Company

www.crabtreebooks.com   1-800-387-7650

Printed in Canada/062017/MA20170420

Published in Canada
Crabtree Publishing
616 Welland Ave.
St. Catharines, Ontario
L2M 5V6

Published in the United States
Crabtree Publishing
PMB 59051
350 Fifth Avenue, 59th Floor
New York, New York 10118

Published in the United Kingdom
Crabtree Publishing
Maritime House
Basin Road North, Hove
BN41 1WR

Published in Australia
Crabtree Publishing
3 Charles Street
Coburg North
VIC 3058

Contents

BEING CAREFUL WITH YOUR CASH

Ah, the money tree! Everyone wishes they had one, but unfortunately money doesn't grow on trees. If it did, we would all be rich. Only a small percentage of the world is fabulously wealthy. The rest of the people on the planet have to be careful with the cash they earn and spend. When your parents tell you, "You need to learn the value of a dollar," they mean you should know how much work it takes to earn a dollar. Knowing it and living it are two different things.

For Richer or Poorer ...

There's an old saying, "Look after the pennies, and the pounds will look after themselves." A pound is a British unit of money similar to a dollar. The saying means if you are careful and don't waste small amounts of money (the pennies), small savings will turn into large savings (the pounds). World currencies may vary, but the idea of building wealth from a small amount to a larger amount is the same around the world. You have to start somewhere, so you might as well start with learning the value of money.

Money Matters

So what is the value of money? The term itself has several meanings. It can mean the actual value of the dollar on a financial market, or how much one dollar will buy. Say you want to buy your favorite basketball shoes. They cost $200. You earn $40 on weekends doing odd jobs for a neighbor. That means you have to work five weekends to pay for one pair of shoes. Is the cost worth your time and effort? What if you also want a night out—wearing your new shoes, of course? Can you afford to go to a movie in addition to buying the shoes? How long will it take you to save enough to go out, too? Will you save it piggybank-style or will you open a bank account at a nearby bank? There are so many questions to answer to make just one purchase.

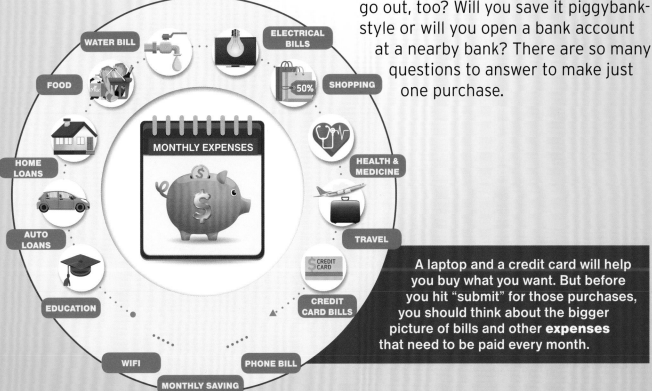

WATER BILL
ELECTRICAL BILLS
FOOD
50% SHOPPING
MONTHLY EXPENSES
HOME LOANS
HEALTH & MEDICINE
AUTO LOANS
TRAVEL
EDUCATION
CREDIT CARD
CREDIT CARD BILLS
WIFI
PHONE BILL
MONTHLY SAVING

A laptop and a credit card will help you buy what you want. But before you hit "submit" for those purchases, you should think about the bigger picture of bills and other **expenses** that need to be paid every month.

Sharpen Your Financial Smarts

Rather than going through life worrying, feeling guilty, and experiencing jealousy, you can have a healthier relationship with your dollars and cents. You can choose to sharpen your money smarts. This area of expertise is called financial literacy, and it's something you can start working on right now.

We live in an age of information, and there's a lot to learn and talk about! Making money a part of the conversation of everyday life is a big step on the path to financial literacy and success.

Learn the Language of Money

Financial literacy is about learning the language of money and becoming comfortable speaking that language. It's about understanding how to earn money, keep track of it, and save and spend it wisely. Mostly, financial literacy is about learning how money works and how it can work for you.

Many people consider money a **taboo** subject or something that is not acceptable to talk about in public. Not talking about money, though, is one of the things that can lead to financial problems in life.

$PEAKING OF MONEY ...

"Young people must develop a positive relationship with money and learn that their relationship with money is a life skill and as important as their relationship with language, reading, or arithmetic. They need to learn that money is actually a tool to help them achieve what they want in life."

Financial Planning Standards Council
(Canada), 2011

Off to a Good Start

At this moment, you might not have a lot of cash of your own, and the adults in your life probably look after the family finances. Chances are you've never given much thought to money. Why start now when you probably don't even have much?

The reality is that right now is the perfect time in your life to start learning about money, because you can build good habits before you start earning money. As you move into your teenage years, you're going to start craving cash so you can go out with friends more often, buy cool stuff, and maybe even save for something big. In adulthood, the demands on your money will become even more mind-boggling. Eventually, you'll have bills to pay, groceries to buy, and maybe even kids to put through college. Whew!

By becoming financially literate now, you'll know exactly how to handle your wealth when life gets more complicated.

Of course, before you can start managing money, you need to have some money to manage. Everyone knows money doesn't grow on trees. So where does it come from?

As a young person, your interests and responsibilities require fewer financial decisions than you will have as an adult. Still, now is a good time to begin developing financial literacy. So earn, learn, plan now—and avoid feeling guilt and stressing about money later.

GREED IS NOT GOOD

For some people, money isn't a positive thing. We often believe that money and power go hand in hand. People with more money often have more influence, or authority, because people perceive them to be important.

For some people, no amount of money will ever be enough. These people crave the power and admiration that comes with being rich. Sometimes, they do terrible things to line their pockets. Greed becomes their motivator.

Some might steal from family members, underpay **employees**, or cheat their friends. But others take it even further. They might do illegal, harmful, and **unethical** things in the name of money. For example, they might kill endangered animals, such as tigers, rhinos, or elephants, and sell the animals' skins or tusks. They might sell drugs. Or they might convince hundreds of innocent people to hand over their hard-earned dollars with promises to make that money grow—then they vanish with the cash.

Greed can drive some people to behave in nasty, hurtful, and dangerous ways. It's important to recognize **fraud** and avoid it. It's also important to recognize the negative effects of greed in yourself to help you maintain a healthy relationship with money.

CHAPTER TWO

WORKING HARD FOR THE MONEY

Some people are fortunate to be born into wealthy families. Others might marry wealthy people. A handful of people might even win a lottery—although you're at least 10 times more likely to be hit by a meteorite falling to Earth than to win a jackpot. For the record, the odds of being struck by a meteorite are one in one-and-a-half million. That makes the chances of winning the lottery one in 15 million. But most of us don't have money handed to us on a silver platter. Those who are able to work earn most of their money themselves. One way to do that is to get a job.

Another Day, Another Dollar

Most people with jobs work hard for their money. They get jobs to earn **income**, so they can pay for the things they want and need in life, and also to be able to help others and contribute to their communities.

Jobs can be full time (35 to 40 hours a week), or part time (fewer weekly hours). They are often long term, or "permanent," but sometimes companies hire people for short-term **contracts**. A contract position is one that lasts for a pre-set period of time, usually a number of weeks or months. Another type of work is called "casual," or "**on-call**." This means workers are called in if they are needed, and don't have a regular schedule of hours or days when they work.

Some employees earn an hourly **wage**. They are paid for the number of hours they work. Others bring in a **salary**–a fixed amount of money that doesn't change no matter how many hours they work.

What Would You Do?

TO WORK OR NOT TO WORK?

Here's an interesting statistic: Since the 1990s, the percentage of teenagers who work during the school year and summers has steadily declined. It's hard to know just what has led to this trend.

Perhaps there are fewer part-time jobs available than there used to be. It's also worth considering the reasons why teens might decide not to work. They might not have transportation to get to a job. Working part-time to bring in money also means making sacrifices of time. Teens must consider whether the amount of personal time a job takes, including transportation time, is a worthwhile trade-off for the amount of money they will earn. Also, taking a job often means having to give up a weekly

How Kids Make $

You might be earning a salary without even realizing it. Almost 80 percent of parents and caregivers in North America give their children a weekly allowance. Most of those adults expect their children to do chores around the house in exchange for that allowance. In effect, that is a salary—a set amount of money in exchange for a specific type of work.

Until you turn 14, working for your allowance is one of the few jobs you are allowed to have in the United States. To protect children from **exploitation**, or being treated badly in the workplace, governments in most countries have established child labor laws. According to U.S. laws, the only paid jobs children under age 14 are permitted to do are to deliver newspapers, babysit, and work as an actor or performer in movies, TV, or theater. They are also allowed to work for their parents in a family business. Similar laws exist in Canada, where the individual provinces and territories restrict the employment of children in their early to mid-teens.

That's not to say children can't earn money in other ways. Nothing prevents kids from starting their own businesses—something to think about if you're ready to bring in a little extra moolah.

Babysitting and working in a family business are two jobs that kids might be allowed to have before they are old enough for regular work.

allowance from parents. Other sacrifices might be giving up time spent doing things that are important to teenagers. These things might include spending time with family and friends, as well as finding time for homework, sports, volunteer work, and other after-school activities.

It's important to remember that some teens do not have a choice. Many have to work to help bring in money to pay for their families' household expenses. But for teens able to choose, it seems that fewer are choosing to work. Could it be that more young people are deciding that making money is less important to them than spending time with their family and friends, or doing other important things...including just having fun?

What do you think? And what choice do you think you'd make?

THINK FOR YOURSELF

To Work or Not to Work? Consider the Trade-Offs

What kinds of trade-offs do we make when we get a job after school or during the summer?

Make a list of the positives and negatives of being a teenager with a job. Then make another list of the positives and negatives of being a teenager without a job.

Ask your friends or classmates what they think about these lists, and what, if anything, they might add to them.

	TEENAGER WITH A JOB	TEENAGER WITHOUT A JOB
POSITIVES	Having a regular income	Income from allowance
	Build job experience	More time for extra-curricular activities
	Have money to buy things I need and want	Summers and school vacation time off
NEGATIVES	Summers and school vacations spent working	Not having enough money for things I need
	Less time for extra-curricular activities	Not building job experience, which may make it difficult to get a future job

F⊙CUS ON FINANCE

For Your Own Good

Most countries have child labor laws to protect young people. The goal of these laws is to make sure employers don't take advantage of children and teens or put them in harm's way.

Child labor laws usually lay out the types of jobs and number of hours young people are allowed to work. Typically, these laws also prevent an employer from interfering with a student's education. Teens between 14 and 16 are usually not allowed to work during school hours.

Child labor laws also restrict locations where youth can work, along with materials they can work with. For example, teenagers between 16 and 18 may be able to work unlimited hours, but they would not be permitted to work in an underground mine, or with harmful or toxic materials.

Some labor laws might sound limiting, but they have been put in place for your protection—to make sure you and your friends are treated fairly, while working in safe environments.

F⊙CUS ON FINANCE

Asking for a Raise

When people in the working world feel that they deserve a higher hourly wage or salary, they often request an increase in the money they are paid. This is called asking for a **raise**. To get a raise, an employee—or a group that represents many employees, such as a labor union—presents reasons to convince the boss to pay more money. Reasons might include keeping up with the rising **cost of living**, in exchange for added responsibilities, or because the employee's work is exceptional.

What Would You Do?

IS A RAISE IN YOUR FUTURE?

Most parents expect kids to work for their allowances. For example, you might have to clean your room, load the dishwasher, and walk the dog every day to earn your weekly salary.

If you wanted to save for something special, how would you ask the adults in your life to agree to bump up your allowance? Do you think the best approach might be to talk about the value of the work you are already doing? Could you also suggest adding new chores to your list of duties? What extra tasks might you be willing to perform to earn extra income?

Is a "DIY" Career Path for You?

Getting a job is not the only way to earn money. Some people choose to be self-employed, which means that they work for themselves. A person who establishes and runs his or her own business is called an **entrepreneur**.

The upside of being an entrepreneur is that you're in charge of how your business runs, you get to keep all of the **profits**, and you set your own schedule for when and where you work. That all sounds pretty sweet!

Unfortunately, running a business isn't quite that simple. If it were, everyone might be doing it!

Being an entrepreneur also has its downsides. People who are self-employed usually work longer hours than people who work for others.

It can also be stressful being the only person responsible for making all the decisions. If you have ever had a lemonade stand, you know how it feels to have to sit by the side of the road, often by yourself, with all the responsibility for providing the product and lots of time on your hands with little money coming in.

That is, of course, a very simple example, and you can decide any time you want to pack up your lemonade stand and go home! Packing up isn't always an option for entrepreneurs. In the adult world, if the business doesn't make money, neither does the business owner. It can be a risky way of life, and not everyone is cut out to be an entrepreneur.

THE PRICE OF CONVENIENCE

When you get a job, you'll start receiving regular paychecks. Like most people who are paid a salary or a wage, you will probably have a checking or savings account at your local bank. You can deposit your paychecks there in person, or have them electronically transferred into your account by your employer.

When you need cash, you have several ways of **withdrawing** money from your account. Before the invention of **ATMs** (Automated, or Automatic, Teller Machines), most people cashed their checks or withdrew money from their bank in person. You can still do this today, but there are also other ways of getting cash.

Some people who may not have a checking or savings account, or who need money when the banks are closed, cash their paychecks at check-cashing stores. These can be independent shops or special service counters within other stores. Check-cashing services are convenient, but they are costly. They usually charge a **flat fee** plus a percentage of the check amount. It's important to ask about these costs before you hand over your check.

Another risk of using these stores is that criminals know the people leaving them often have a pocketful of money. For this reason, it's important never to visit a check-cashing service alone, and never one in a place, or at a time of day or night, that makes you feel uncomfortable.

For decades, ATMs have been a popular way of withdrawing money. Even if you've never used an ATM, you've probably seen adults use them, either on TV and in the movies, or in real life. With a credit card or **debit card** issued by your bank, you can get cash from your account.

As convenient as ATMs are, there are costs for using them that you may not know about. The most common cost is a fee that may be charged to your account simply for using the ATM.

In addition to these costs, the same warning about keeping you and your money safe applies to ATMs as to check-cashing stores. You should be especially careful to avoid using an ATM in a place or at a time that might put you at risk of being robbed or attacked.

BECOME YOUR OWN BOSS

Give It a Try, and DIY

If you think you might be an entrepreneur-in-the-making, now is a good time to test that theory. Make sure that you talk to an adult first. She or he can help you get started, support you along the way, and make sure you're being safe.

1. Make a list of things you like to do, things you're good at, and things you can make or build. For example, you might be good at drawing.

2. For each item on your list, brainstorm with adults or friends about how you could turn that skill, service, or product into a business. If you're good at drawing, for example, perhaps you could design and sell greeting cards.

3. Test your idea. Ask friends, schoolmates, and family members if they would pay for the product or service you want to offer. How much would they pay for one of your greeting cards, for example?

4. Determine how much it would cost you to start your business, where you would get that start-up money, whether you have enough after-school time to run the business, and how you would find customers. If you're going to make greeting cards, how much would the materials cost? How long would it take to make each card? Who would you sell cards to?

5. After you have considered all these things and come up with solutions that work, try it out. You might discover that you have the entrepreneurial spirit!

The Right Entrepreneurial Stuff

It takes certain personality traits to be a successful entrepreneur. Self-discipline and self-confidence are among the most important qualities. Self-discipline means that a person is able to work hard and stick to a schedule. An entrepreneur also needs to have the money smarts to make the business work. Having an adventurous spirit doesn't hurt either!

If you think you might have the right personality to become an entrepreneur, now is a good time to try it out. If you are a young person living at home, you probably still have some financial support from adults. They might also be willing to help you start your business.

A World of Possibilities!

The first thing you need to do to launch your new **enterprise** is come up with a great idea. You might choose to start with opening that lemonade stand or starting a dog-walking or car-washing business. You could provide a service to homeowners by raking leaves in the fall, shoveling snow in the winter, and gardening and mowing grass in the spring and summer. Or, you could invent and sell a new product.

Start by aking yourself what you're good at. What are your interests and hobbies? What could you make or provide that another person might pay for?

BE CAREFUL OUT THERE

DON'T GO IT ALONE

If you decide to earn a little extra money, make sure the adults in your life are involved. They are responsible for you until you grow up, and they need to know about and approve important decisions such as starting a moneymaking activity. It's important that they know how you are earning money, how much money you are making, and who you are working with to earn that income. They can also help you decide what to do with your money once you've earned it.

For example, if you love to read, perhaps you could offer a read-aloud service to people who are older or visually impaired. Are you a computer whiz? Maybe adults who aren't so tech **savvy** would pay you to set up their devices, or tutor them on the latest software. Do you have musical or acting talent? Think about putting on a play or concert and charging admission.

If you have a good idea, support from your family, and a willingness to take a chance, you're already well on your way to entrepreneurial excellence!

The Ins and Outs of Income

Sources of income can be divided into three categories: active income, **passive income**, and **portfolio** income.

Active Income

Active, or earned, income, is the money you get for work you do. If you stop working, you no longer have an active income. Earnings from self-employment also fall into the active income category. If your business shuts down, so does the flow of income.

Do you have great language, math, social studies, science, or computer skills? Put them to use as a source of active income by tutoring kids or adults in areas that are among your strengths.

Passive Income

The second type of income, passive income, is money you earn after you've stopped working on a project. Usually, you have to spend a lot of time or energy to begin earning passive income. Once it has started, though, it keeps on giving.

For example, if you write a book, you might later get a **royalty**, or part of the profits, from every copy of the book sold. Another example of passive income is money earned from renting out living space to others. Say your parents buy a house, but your family doesn't live in it. Instead, your parents rent the house out to **tenants**—people who pay rent every month for the privilege of living there. Your parents are called **landlords**. The monthly rent the tenants pay is passive income for your parents.

Once someone has set up a passive money-making plan, they still have to keep track of money made and spent. They also have to be sure that certain services are provided. For example, a landlord has to take care of rental properties by doing repairs or yard work, to keep earning money from tenants.

Royalties are payments based on the sale of books and other creative products, such as music, movie scripts, and inventions. For a best-selling author like Kim Harrison (shown here on the right), royalties are a significant source of passive income made well after her work has been completed and published. The royalty payments may be based on the sale of both printed books and ebook editions which people read on computers and other electronic devices.

Sources of Passive Income: High-Tech and Not-So-High-Tech

As a young person, you might not be allowed to have a part-time job yet, but something you *are* allowed to do is create a source of passive income for yourself. That's money you can earn after you're done creating something!

If, for example, you have tech talent, or learn high-tech skills in the future, you might develop a new app, start a YouTube channel, or create a blog or podcast. People could pay to use your app or view your content. Or, advertisers might give you money to show ads on your videos or websites. These are all potential sources of passive income. If this interests you, ask an adult such as a teacher or member of your family to help you get started. You'll have to put in some work to establish your site or app and attract followers!

Maybe you're more of a low-tech type. Do you have a great comic book collection? Maybe other comic-book lovers would pay to borrow your books. If so, you could start a comic book library. You'd have to do some work upfront, such as collecting the comics, organizing a check-out system, and advertising your new library. Once that work is done, and kids start paying fees to borrow your books, you'll have to keep track of your comics and the money you're making—but you'll have set yourself up with a source of passive income!

Portfolio Income

The third type of income is called portfolio, or **investment**, income. This probably isn't something you'll be doing any time soon. It takes a fair bit of money to start the process, and it can be a risky way to bring in the bucks. Still, now is a good time to learn about portfolio income. That way, later in life, when you have money in the bank, you'll know how to make it work for you.

bonds funds cash financial currency

securities risk

contribution

INVESTMENT

income estate future economics resources

management debt deposit

IT TAKES MONEY TO MAKE MONEY

Of the three types of income an individual can earn—active, passive, or portfolio—the last one on the list is the most complex. That's because portfolio, or investment, income includes all kinds of possibilities and options. Each of the opportunities comes with a particular set of **risks and rewards,** or returns. Despite the differences, they all have two things in common:

1. They all require money up front.

2. They rarely earn instant income.

Buy Low, Sell High

It can take years, or even decades, for some investments to make money. The goal is to invest, or pay money, now to make lots of money later! A person can invest in many different ways. It's important to understand these options before any cash changes hands.

Some people choose to invest in a single long-term opportunity, but experts say it's wiser not to put all your eggs in one basket. It's a good idea to **diversify**, or divide your money among a variety of options. That way, if one investment does badly, you'll have others to help make up for it. A person's set of investments is called a portfolio. Each investment in that portfolio has the potential to put money in the buyer's pocket—but different types of investments earn different types of money.

A common way to earn portfolio income is to buy and sell things. This might sound easy. A person buys something, holds onto it for a while, and later sells it for more money than he or she originally paid for it. Unfortunately, it's not quite that simple. How do people know what to buy and when to sell? How do they know something will increase in value? How do they make sure they don't lose all their money?

RISKY BUSINESS

Choosing where to invest money for the long term is about balancing risk and reward (or risk and return). Usually, the lower the risk, the lower the financial payout, or reward, over time. An investor who chooses a low-risk option will likely make money, just not a lot of it. Higher-risk opportunities usually come with the chance to earn greater, or faster, payoffs–but they also come with a greater chance of losing money.

Decisions about where to invest money for the long term vary from individual to individual. What is right for one person is not necessarily the best choice for another person. It's important for each investor to consider his or her own situation, weigh the options, and decide how much risk they are willing to take. Each individual can then make the best choices for their personal situation.

What to Buy and Sell?

Almost anything can be purchased and sold. But not everything that can be bought and sold makes a good investment. Here are some places where investors often choose to put their money.

Real Estate

One of the safest and most popular purchases to include in an investment portfolio is **real estate**. This type of investment involves buying houses, apartment buildings, land, or **commercial properties** (land or buildings for businesses). Real estate investment has two potential income streams: passive and portfolio.

If a person buys a property and rents it out, that person earns passive income in the form of regular rent payments from tenants.

Investing in real estate can also be an excellent source of portfolio income. Over time, many factors can make property more valuable. These include increases in population, which create a higher demand for buildings and land; improvements that enhance property values; and changes in neighboring properties that increase the appeal of land and buildings around them.

At some point, the owner might choose to sell the property. The goal is to keep the real estate until it is worth significantly more than what the owner bought it for. That way, the owner makes money on the investment.

In some cases, real estate can lose value over time. More often, though, it increases in price. So even though buying property might mean spending a lot of money upfront, it is usually considered a wise investment.

Buying and selling real estate can be a great way to earn money as your property increases in value. It's important, however, to include the costs of electricity and other **utilities**, as well as repairs, maintenance, and improvements, in your decision to buy real estate. You will have to pay these expenses, plus **taxes** on the value of your property, for as long as you own it.

Collections and Collectibles

Instead of buying buildings, some investors choose to invest their money in valuable objects or collections. Stamp, coin, and art collections are popular items to purchase. Other buyers invest in individual items, or **collectibles**, rather than entire collections of things. They might purchase a rare comic book, a painting by a famous artist, or an outfit once worn by a famous actor, in hopes that the item will increase in value over time.

Buying and selling collections and collectibles is one of the riskiest types of investments out there. It is impossible to know when, or if, that antique clock, autographed baseball, or doll collection will increase in value. It all depends on public tastes and trends that can't be easily predicted.

FOCUS ON FINANCE

What's in Your Attic?

You never know what might have value one day. Believe it or not, some hard-to-find Lego sets are now worth thousands of dollars. An original 1998 Furby could be worth several hundred dollars today. A few years ago, a 1979 Wayne Gretzky rookie hockey card sold for more than $94,000! Some toys, such as Cabbage Patch Kids and Shopkins figures, may not be particularly rare. They are still highly valued as collectibles, however, so they often sell at higher prices. It might be worth taking a look in your attic, closets, and basement to see what you can find!

Stocks

Another item people commonly purchase in hopes of earning portfolio income is stock in a business. Stocks are shares, or units of ownership, in a company. Stocks are traded, or bought and sold, on a **stock market**. The reason a company would sell shares to members of the public is to raise cash for things they need, such as a new office building, research, or a new project.

When a person buys stocks in a company, he or she joins thousands of other investors. Each investor owns a tiny piece of the business. That doesn't mean the investors get a say in how the company is run. Instead, they get a share of the profits if the company does well. On the other hand, if the company loses money, so do the investors, or shareholders. The way an investor earns money from stocks is the same way a homebuyer earns money—by waiting until the value of the stock increases, then selling it for more money than they paid for it in the first place.

Stock prices change every day. Sometimes it's tempting to sell stocks that are falling in value. The key to buying and selling stocks, though, is to hold onto them for a long time and wait out the ups and downs. Typically, over long periods of time, stock prices rise—but there are no guarantees.

Another way a person might earn income from certain stocks is through **dividends**. A dividend is a piece of the profits that a company pays to shareholders several times a year. This is a regular amount of money that shareholders will receive. Not all stocks pay dividends.

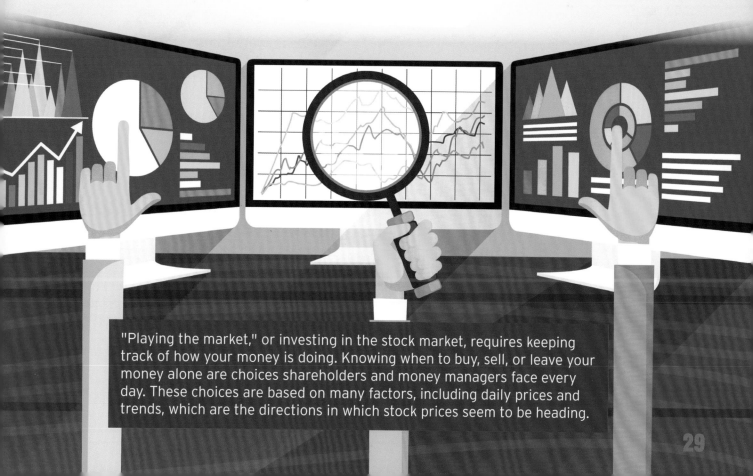

"Playing the market," or investing in the stock market, requires keeping track of how your money is doing. Knowing when to buy, sell, or leave your money alone are choices shareholders and money managers face every day. These choices are based on many factors, including daily prices and trends, which are the directions in which stock prices seem to be heading.

PLAY THE MARKET *

Company Name & Symbol	DAY 1		DAY 2		DAY 13		DAY 14	
	price per share	price per 100 shares	price per share	price per 100 shares	price per share	price per 100 shares	price per share	price per 100 shares
Apple AAPL	$131.33	$13,133	$129.55	$12,955	$132.20	$13,220	$131.99	$13,199
Clean Energy Fuel Corp CLNE	$2.56	$256	$3.55	$355	$3.54	$354	$3.60	$360
Microsoft MSFT	$64.97	$6,497	$67.83	$6,783	$62.03	$6,203	$63.10	$6,310
Portfolio (total)								

* All prices are fictitious. Due to space restrictions, three companies only are represented, and Days 3–12 are omitted.

Give It a Try, and DIY

PLAY THE MARKET

Have you ever heard of playing the stock market? It's a way to describe investing money in stocks. The goal of investing in the stock market is to make money, but it also involves the risk of losing money. Investing in stocks is a balancing act between risks and rewards, or losses and gains. The goal is to tip the balance in your favor so you make a profit. Following stocks in the market before you put money in is a good way to learn about the ups and downs of investing. You're going to use imaginary money, so in this case playing the market really is like playing a game. In this game, you have nothing to lose! Here we go:

1. **Choose six companies that interest you.** These might include fast-food restaurants, the organization that makes your favorite game, or a brand of clothing. Not all companies sell shares, so your favorite store may not appear on the stock market.

2. **Search online for the stock, or ticker, symbol each company uses on the stock market.** Most symbols are three- or four-letter codes. For example, AAPL is the symbol for Apple Inc., the computer company.

BUY PRICE (Day 1)	SELL PRICE (Day 14)	PROFIT OR LOSS (PROFIT +, LOSS -)
$13,133	$13,199	+$66
$256	$360	+$104
$6,497	$6,310	-$187
$_____	$_____	+ or - $_____

3. Create a chart with rows beginning with the name and symbol of each company. Leave enough space after the name of each company for columns tracking information from Day 1 through Day 14 (two weeks).

4. Track the price of those stocks every day for two weeks, as in the example above:

   a. On Day 1, find the price of 1 unit of each company's stock. You can do this online. For example, a web search for "AAPL stock price" will give you the current cost of 1 share of Apple. Record that number.

   b. Using imaginary money, "buy" 100 shares of each company on Day 1. How much does that cost? Record the amount for each stock.

   c. Repeat this procedure for all six stocks every day for two weeks, writing down how much it would cost to buy 100 shares every day.

   d. On the final day of tracking, "sell" all of your stocks. How much money did you make—or lose—on each company?

5. Look at how the stock prices changed during the two-week period. Did the price of each stock go up or down? Did you make or lose imaginary money on each stock? How much? Based on this information, determine which stocks were good investments for you.

6. How much money did your entire "portfolio" make or lose over the two weeks? Compare the total price of all 6 companies' shares on Day 1 with the total price on Day 14.

Spread the Wealth

Buying and selling things isn't the only way to earn portfolio income. Other investments pay in different ways, and each comes with its own set of risks and rewards.

Bonds

Bonds are one of the most popular additions to an investment portfolio. Governments issue bonds when they need to raise money. Citizens who buy bonds agree to loan the government money for a fixed period of time. When the time is up, the government pays the money back. In the meantime, the government also pays **interest** to the bond-buyers for the privilege of using their money. Interest is a fee a person or organization pays when they have borrowed money.

Government-issued bonds are considered safe investments because buyers know they will eventually get their money back, with interest. Some corporations also issue bonds. These are considered riskier purchases for investors, because private businesses take more risks to make money than governments do. Corporations can lose money or be unable to repay investors.

Bonds

There's never any guarantee as to how successful any investment will be. If chosen carefully, however, bonds are generally considered among the safest investments. They don't pay a lot of interest, but they usually carry fewer risks than stocks, whose value can rise and fall unpredictably.

Open a bank account

Enter

sign up now for more privileges

F⊙CUS ON FINANCE

Money in the Bank

The simplest, safest place to invest your money is in a bank account. Banks pay interest on the money their customers deposit. Interest is a fee a person or organization pays for the privilege of using someone else's money. As long as you have money in the bank, you'll earn interest, and your money will grow.

A bank is a safe place to put your dollars and cents, but the **return on investment** (the amount your money grows) is very low. Right now, **interest rates** are so minimal that you won't earn much extra. That's why many people look for other places to invest their hard-earned dollars.

Bank

shares at a higher price than they were originally bought for. This works because mutual funds rise and fall in value, similar to stocks.

Yes, It Can Get Complicated!

When you're ready to invest your money, real estate, stocks, bonds, and mutual funds are some of the first products you'll likely consider.

There are many other options, too, and there are options within each of the options. It can be complicated! The important thing is to do your research, and make sure you understand what you're getting into before you take chances with your money.

MUTUAL FUNDS

Mutual funds are another common portfolio purchase. These are collections of stocks, bonds, and other investment products overseen, or run, by a fund manager. Fund managers collect cash from a large group of individuals, then decide how to invest that collective stash of cash. Mutual funds allow individuals to buy into a greater variety of investments than they could do on their own.

Mutual funds earn financial rewards in different ways, depending on their contents. Some pay dividends (a share of the profits) and interest (the fee paid to shareholders for using their money). Sometimes, the fund manager sells some of the fund's contents at a profit, and passes this on to shareholders. To sell contents at a profit, the fund manager sells

$PEAKING OF MONEY ...

"The successful investors I know have learned to manage their own money rather than let someone else do it for them. They keep it simple and avoid anything they don't understand."

John Heinzl, investment columnist, *The Globe and Mail* newspaper, 2016

BE CAREFUL OUT THERE

WINNING AND LOSING: NO SUCH THING AS A SURE BET

Believe it or not, according to some reports, about 20 percent of Americans were counting on "winning the lottery" to finance their retirement plans. Even more incredibly, in another survey, about 34 percent—more than one-third—of Canadians included "winning the lottery" in their long-term financial plans. Given the extremely low odds of winning a jackpot, this is a losing **strategy**—and a big risk for a person's future. Why, then, is it OK to take risks on long-term investment options?

There is a big difference between investment risk and gambling. With gambling, you have no way to influence the outcome. For example, you put your money into a slot machine, push the button, and the machine decides whether you win or lose. You don't get a say in it.

On the other hand, when you take a risk, you do your homework first, consider and assess the options, and make educated choices. If a financial risk isn't paying off, you can take your money out, and move it elsewhere. Of course, there are no guarantees that any investment will pay off, but with research, careful monitoring, and understanding how money works, you can increase the odds of success.

CHAPTER FOUR

REALITY CHECKS

Whether you get a job, start a business, or buy investments, the good news is you'll earn money during your lifetime. The bad news is that you won't get to keep all of it. State (or provincial) and federal governments take part of your earnings, to help keep the country running. The money that they take is called taxes. Don't be shocked when you receive your first paycheck and see that your **take-home pay** is less than you actually earned. Giving to the government, in the form of taxes and other contributions, is a fact of life.

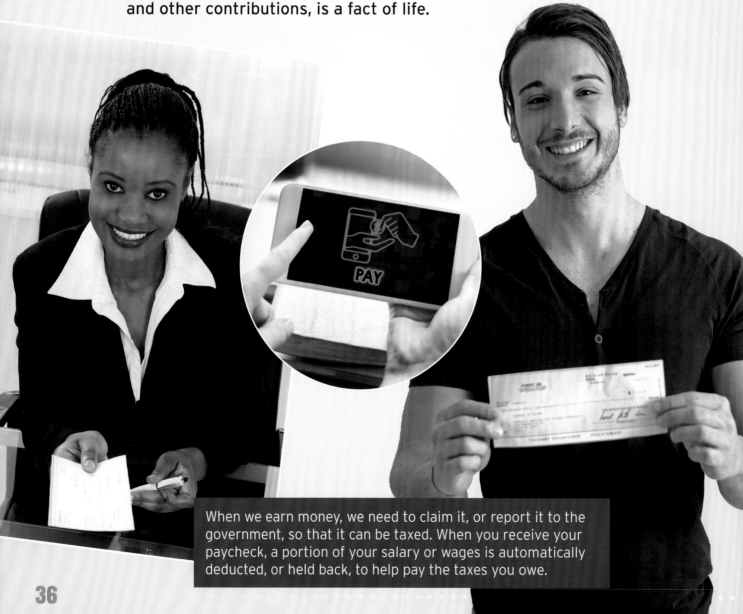

When we earn money, we need to claim it, or report it to the government, so that it can be taxed. When you receive your paycheck, a portion of your salary or wages is automatically deducted, or held back, to help pay the taxes you owe.

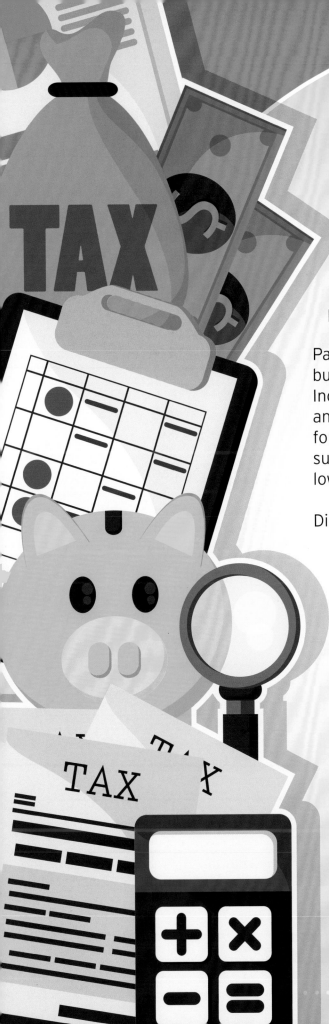

Sharing the Wealth

Income tax is something you'll become very familiar with as you grow up. All your earnings, wherever they come from, will be taxed. In addition to taxes paid to the federal government, citizens in the United States also pay taxes to their state governments. Citizens in Canada also pay taxes to their provincial governments.

Paying taxes is something everyone growls about, but it's one of the ways governments raise money. Income taxes help pay for schools, health care, and other social programs. The money is also used for public safety initiatives, national defense, and support for citizens who are elderly or who have low incomes or special needs.

Different countries have different formulas, or ways to figure out how much tax each person has to pay. These formulas can be quite complicated, and the rules change regularly—just to keep you on your toes! What you need to know right now, so you're not surprised later, is that employers are required to hold back a portion of their employees' income for government taxes. They deduct those dollars from your paycheck before you even see them.

Every person who earns money is required to file a yearly income **tax return**. This tells the government how much tax each individual is supposed to pay, based on how much money they make and some of their expenses. If you pay all your taxes for the year through your employer, you won't have to pay any more. If you've paid too much tax during the year, the government will give you a refund. If you haven't paid your share, you will get a bill for more.

TRACK YOUR BUCKS

Give It a Try, and DIY

Right now, you may have just one or two sources of income. Still, it's a good idea to keep track of exactly how much money you make, so you know how much you have for spending—and for saving. Eventually, you will be required to document your earnings for income tax purposes, so it's a good habit to get into as soon as money starts coming your way:

1. Make a chart of all of your sources of income. Include allowance, birthday money, scholarships, and any other money that comes in.

    a. In column 1, write the date you received the money.

    b. In column 2, write the source of the money (birthday, other gift, etc.).

    c. In column 3, write the amount of money you received.

2. In columns 4 and 5, keep a running total of your money as it comes in, and your total income every month. This will allow you to see clearly how much money you've earned every month. It will also help you see if there are any patterns to the way your money comes in.

DATE	SOURCE	AMOUNT RECEIVED	TOTAL RECEIVED TO DATE	TOTAL FOR MONTH
Jan. 24	Allowance	$5.00	$5.00	
Jan. 29	Snow shoveling	$10.00	$15.00	
Jan. 31	Allowance	$5.00	$20.00	$20.00 (Jan.)
Feb. 7	Allowance	$5.00	$25.00	
Feb. 14	Allowance	$5.00	$30.00	
Feb. 21	Allowance	$5.00	$35.00	
Feb. 22	Snow shoveling	$10.00	$45.00	
Feb. 28	Allowance	$5.00	$50.00	$30.00 (Feb.)

Before You Spend All Your Cash ...

People with jobs are not the only ones who pay income tax. Entrepreneurs—those who work for themselves—must also contribute. They are required to keep track of all their income and pay taxes on their annual earnings. Self-employed people can lower their incomes by deducting, or subtracting, the costs of running their businesses.

Say, for example, you earn money by selling hand-made greeting cards. To make those cards and operate your business, you have to buy pens, paper, envelopes, stickers, and other supplies. You can deduct the costs of those items from your total income.

If you earned $500 from your greeting card business one year, and spent $200 on supplies, your taxable income would be $300. Of course, this is a small example.

Income tax would not be applied on an amount this low. Everyone is allowed to make a certain amount of money (usually around $10,000-11,000) before income tax kicks in.

People who earn passive and portfolio income also pay taxes on their annual earnings.

Paying taxes might sound unfair now. But, as you grow older, you'll be more aware of what your tax dollars do, such as fixing roads, running public swimming pools, and helping you out if you become unemployed. It's something everyone does to receive benefits and help support their fellow citizens.

THINK FOR YOURSELF

Add up the Numbers...

After logging your income for several months, look at the income numbers. Think about these questions:

- Does the amount change from month to month?
- If so, are there patterns relating to when your income increases or decreases?
- Is your monthly income enough to cover your spending and saving, or do you run out of money by the end of the month?
- If so, is it time to start thinking about ways to add to your income?

Lessons Learned

In this book, you've learned about three different types of income.

Active income is money earned through a job or self-employment. This is the money that comes in as long as an individual is working. Passive income is money that continues to flow in, even after work on something has finished. This might include royalties from a book you've written or sales of an app you've developed. The third type of income, portfolio income, is money you earn later on investments.

Understanding how to bring in a steady supply of dollars and cents is crucial—but it's only part of your financial literacy training. It's also important to learn what to do with all the income you're going to bring in during your lifetime.

More than half of American adults spend all the cash they bring in as soon as they earn it. They don't make plans for their financial futures or keep track of where their hard-earned dollars go. By spending their money this way, they are not able to get ahead, save for something special, or plan for emergency situations. It's a frustrating—and financially risky—way to live.

The best way to make sure you don't fall into this so-called **paycheck-to-paycheck** lifestyle is to learn money management skills today.

Contributing to the Community

When you receive your first paycheck, you will see a list of numbers. These show the total amount of money you've earned, along with several **deductions**.

Deductions are amounts subtracted from your earned income to help pay for government-funded services, organizations, and social programs. In Canada, in addition to income tax, employees pay into the Canada Pension Plan (to support the elderly) and Employment Insurance (to support unemployed people). In the United States, payroll deductions include income tax, a Social Security tax (to support retired people, including you someday), and a Medicare tax (to provide medical care to people over age 65 and to younger people with certain physical disabilities or medical conditions).

The total amount of your earnings is called your **gross income**. The amount you get to take home, after all the deductions have been applied, is called take-home pay, or **net income**.

Don't worry. That's not as complicated or scary as it might sound!

Money management, or financial planning, simply means knowing where your money comes from and where it goes. You've already got a handle on the first half of that equation—you now know about a variety of ways to put money in your pockets. You might even have a business idea or two to try out!

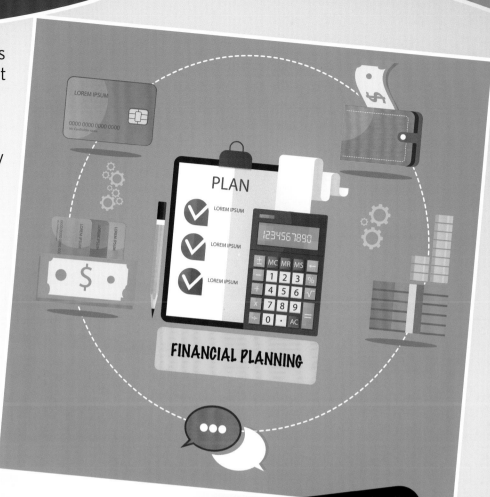

BE CAREFUL OUT THERE

YOU WON'T GET RICH QUICK

"A fool and his (or her) money are soon parted." This is an age-old saying, but it is something that still happens every day. Greedy people take advantage of desperate, poor, or financially unwise people by offering them a way to make a fast buck. These get-rich-quick schemes are scams. They try to tell people that they can suddenly become wealthy by investing a small amount of time or money.

Beware of anything or anyone making such a claim. It is simply not true. There's no such thing as a risk-free, get-rich-quick scheme. Talk to a trusted adult before you give money to anyone.

The next step is to learn what to do with all the money that will be coming and going throughout your life. It's about learning to balance spending and saving. It's about setting realistic financial goals. It's about making sure you have money for today–and for tomorrow.

You're already almost there! Don't stop now. Take the time to learn healthy spending and saving habits. On the next page, you can find some tips about setting financial goals. Check out the other books in this series for in-depth looks at financial planning, spending, and saving.

BE CAREFUL OUT THERE

ON THE HOOK: BUYING AND SELLING MONEY

Another way to bring money into your life is to borrow it. Sometimes, this is a good idea. For example, when people borrow money to buy a house, they gain a long-term benefit from the borrowed money. Sometimes borrowing is a necessity because of a crisis or sudden change in a person's life, such as an illness or losing a job.

Sometimes, though, an individual has to borrow money because of a lack of financial planning or out-of-control spending. That person has to borrow money to pay the bills, feed the family, and survive. This is a dangerous cycle to fall into.

When you borrow money, you pay a fee, called interest. You can think of interest as the price you pay for "buying" money from a lender, who is "selling" it for that fee. The amount of interest, or interest rate, is set by the lender. If you borrow from a bank, for example, the interest rate is fairly low. If, however, you are in **debt** to a credit card company, the interest rate will be sky-high.

The best way to stay out of debt–and avoid paying interest–is to develop your financial literacy skills, plan for your saving and spending, and start becoming money-smart today.

F⊙CUS ON FINANCE
Planning for Tomorrow

A smart financial strategy includes setting saving and spending goals.

Short-term financial goals are things you can achieve with the cash you have on hand. For you, a short-term goal might be to buy a book, go to a movie, or play a round of mini-golf.

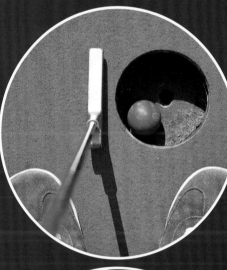

Medium-term financial goals require a bit of saving—maybe a few weeks' allowance. These goals might include such things as purchasing a pair of jeans, a concert ticket, or a gift card for your BFF's birthday.

Long-term financial goals take time to reach. These are expensive items or activities that require weeks or months of saving—a designer outfit, the latest tablet, or an electric guitar, for example.

As you grow up, you will set your sights on even longer-term goals. You might want to save for a college education, a car, or a house. Ultimately, you will also need to save for your retirement.

Right now, that probably sounds like forever-and-a-day into the future—putting it in the long-long-long-term goal category! Certainly, you don't need to start thinking about any of these life-changing targets just yet, but the more you learn about money management now, the better prepared you'll be to cover the costs of these faraway realities later.

GIFT CARD

GLOSSARY

ATM Automated, or Automatic, Teller Machine; a machine that automatically provides cash and performs other financial services to an account holder who uses a credit card or debit card plus a personal security code to gain access to his or her account

collectible An object that a person might buy for a hobby, to display, or to add to a collection

commercial property A property or building that is used for business purposes

contract A written or spoken legal agreement; for employment purposes, a contract sets out the conditions under which one person or company works for another; these conditions may include the number of hours and length of time a person will work, along with the amount of money the person or company will earn for that work

cost of living The amount of money needed to keep up a certain way of living, including such basic costs as food, clothing, housing, and health care; cost of living is often used to compare how expensive it is to live in one place versus another

debit card A bank-issued card that allows the holder to withdraw money or pay for something, directly from his or her bank account

debt Money owed to a person or organization

deduction An amount of money that is subtracted from a person's income

diversify To add variety; to spread an investment over a range of products to lessen the risk of loss

dividend A share of profits that a company pays to people who own stocks in that company

employee A person who works for wages or a salary, usually for a company or for someone at a higher level

enterprise A business or company

entrepreneur A self-employed person who starts and operates a business

expense The amount of money something costs

exploitation Taking advantage of someone, or treating them unfairly

flat fee A set amount that is paid for a service

fraud Using dishonest methods to take something valuable from another person

gross income A person's earned pay before taxes and other deductions are applied

income Money earned or otherwise acquired

income tax A tax, or portion of income, that everyone pays to the government

interest A fee paid to borrow someone else's money

interest rate A portion of an amount owed, usually expressed as a percentage, that determines how much interest is added to the original amount

investment Something that is purchased for the purpose of making money

landlord A person who rents land, a building, work space, or an apartment to a tenant

long-term financial goal Something a person wants to do or buy in the future

medium-term financial goal Something a person wants to do or buy soon but not right away

net income The amount of money a person earns after taxes and other deductions are applied

on-call Having to do with an employee or work situation in which the employee only works when needed and is called in to work

passive income Earnings that continue to come in from a project after it has been completed

paycheck-to-paycheck A situation in which a person or family meets all financial obligations with current earnings from one pay cycle to the next, needing all those earnings to survive until the following payday

portfolio A collection of investments, such as stocks, bonds, and real estate

profit Financial gain; money earned by a company or person, after paying the costs of running the business

raise (money) An increase in income

real estate Land and buildings permanently attached to a piece of land

return on investment The percentage of income earned on an amount of money invested

risk and reward (often called a "risk/reward ratio") A comparison between the risks taken in an activity (such as a price increase) and the profit or return; the risk/reward ratio is used to determine the likelihood of making money on an investment

royalty, royalties A payment made to a writer for each book sold or to a composer of music for each performance or use of the work

salary A set income that doesn't change, regardless of the number of hours a person works

savvy Having practical knowledge, understanding, and ability in a particular area

short-term financial goal Something a person wants to do or buy very soon

stock market A place where shares of companies are bought and sold

strategy A plan for, or approach to, something

taboo Forbidden; prohibited or restricted by social custom

take-home pay The amount of money a person earns after taxes and other deductions are applied; the amount of money a person takes home

tax A fee charged by the government to individuals and businesses based on such factors as income (income tax), the cost of certain items (sales tax), or the value of a house or other real estate (property tax); these charges are used to support the operation of the government and to help pay for services provided by the government

tax return A document that every income-earning person must file each year to declare the total amount of income earned

tenant A person who occupies or uses land or property owned by someone else

unethical Morally, legally, or socially incorrect or improper

utility A service, such as electricity, gas, or water, that is provided to the public; companies that provide such services are also known as utilities, or public utilities

wage A fixed rate of regular payment, usually on an hourly, daily, or weekly basis, made to a worker

withdraw To remove or take away

FURTHER INFORMATION

BOOKS

Dakers, Diane. *The Bottom Line: Money Basics* (Financial Literacy for Life). Crabtree Publishing, 2017.

Merberg, Julie, and Sarah E. Parvis. *How to Start Your Very First Business* (Warren Buffet's Secret Millionaire's Club). Downtown Bookworks, 2015.

Owen, Ruth. *I Can Start a Business!* (Kids Can Do It!). Windmill Books, 2017.

Scheunemann, Pam. *Cool Kids Jobs* (series).   ABDO Publishing, 2011.

WEBSITES

www.youthrules.gov/index.htm
YouthRules!: Preparing the 21st Century Workforce is an important website for American kids interested in getting jobs. It lists all the rules that you and your employer must follow to ensure that you are treated well on the job. It also includes videos, resources, and stories of young people already in the work force.

www.moneyandyouth.cfee.org/en/
This website, called *Money and Youth: A Guide to Financial Literacy*, is produced by the Canadian Foundation for Economic Education. It's great for kids, parents, and teachers who want to learn about finances. It includes a full glossary, links to other sites, and an excellent Q&A section. It also offers a link to a free, and excellent, e-book.

www.smckids.com/
Warren Buffett's *Secret Millionaire's Club* website offers a collection of videos, comic books, and games to help kids learn all about money and finances. Warren is one of the world's most successful and wealthy business executives, so he's worth listening to!

www.themint.org/
The Mint is a website designed to teach financial literacy skills to kids, teens, parents, and teachers. It includes information, games, and tools to help you learn. These three links are good places to start learning about earning money:
www.themint.org/kids/ways-to-invest.html
www.themint.org/kids/earning.html
www.themint.org/teens/earning.html

INDEX

ABOUT THE AUTHOR

Diane Dakers was born and raised in Toronto, and now makes her home in Victoria, British Columbia. She has written three fiction and 18 nonfiction books for young people. During her career, Diane has worked full time, part time, on contract, and on-call. She is currently self-employed. She has earned money in the form of wages, salaries, royalties, scholarships, and investment income. She loves spreadsheets!